Jesus' Parables of Life

James W. Moore

JESUS'
Parables of Life

DIMENSIONS
FOR LIVING
NASHVILLE

JESUS' PARABLES OF LIFE

Copyright © 2005 by Dimensions for Living

All rights reserved.
No part of this work may be reproduced or transmitted in any form or by any means, electronic or mechanical, including photocopying and recording, or by any information storage or retrieval system, except as may be expressly permitted by the 1976 Copyright Act or in writing from the publisher. Requests for permission should be addressed in writing to Dimensions for Living, P.O. Box 801, 201 Eighth Avenue South, Nashville, TN 37202-0801.

This book is printed on acid-free paper.

Library of Congress Cataloging-in-Publication Data

Moore, James W. (James Wendell), 1938-
  Some things are too good not to be true / James W. Moore.
    p. cm.
  ISBN 0-687-06287-X (alk. paper)
  1. Jesus Christ—Teachings. 2. Christian life—Biblical teaching. I. Title.
  BS2415.M59 2005
  248.4—dc22

2004026433

Scripture quotations, unless otherwise noted, are from the New Revised Standard Version of the Bible, copyright © 1989, by the Division of Christian Education of the National Council of the Churches of Christ in the United States of America. Used by permission.

Scripture quotations noted KJV are taken from the King James or Authorized Version of the Bible.

Scripture quotations noted RSV are taken from the Revised Standard Version of the Bible, copyright © 1946, 1952, 1971 by the Division of Christian Education of the National Council of the Churches of Christ in the USA. Used by permission.

05 06 07 08 09 10 11 12 13 14—10 9 8 7 6 5 4 3 2 1

MANUFACTURED IN THE UNITED STATES OF AMERICA

For the members and staff of
St. Luke's United Methodist Church,
Houston, Texas,
with deep gratitude for
their love, their joy,
their prayers,
their encouragement,
their servant leadership,
and their gracious spirit
over the past twenty-one years

CONTENTS

INTRODUCTION

Jesus' Parables of Life

W hy did Jesus use parables, and how do we unravel them and discover their timeless and powerful messages? Let me begin by giving you five key ideas that help unlock the truths found in all the parables of Jesus.

First, Jesus spoke in parables—short stories that teach a moral lesson—to be understood and remembered, to proclaim the good news and make people think.

Second, Jesus saw himself as one who came to serve the needy, and he believed that the kingdom of God existed anywhere kingdom-deeds such as love, mercy, kindness, and compassion were being done.

Third, God's love for us is unconditional, and God wants us to love one another like that—unconditionally.

Fourth, one way to discover the central truth of a parable is to look for the surprise in it. Look for the moment when you lift your eyebrows, or the moment when the original hearers of the story probably thought or said in surprise—or maybe even shock—"Oh my goodness, did you hear that?"

Fifth, it's important to remember that parables are designed to convey one central truth! Parables (as opposed to allegories, in which everything in the story has a symbolic meaning) make one main point.

Parables slip up on us. They flip our values. They turn our world upside down. They surprise us. This is the great thing about the parables of Jesus: They are always relevant and always personal. They speak eloquently to you and me, here and now. In this book, we will examine six of Jesus' thought-provoking parables of life to see if we can find ourselves, and God's truth for us, in these magnificent truth-stories. They are, after all, truth-stories for us—truth-stories from the mind of Jesus that can touch us, enrich us, inspire us, and change our lives as they proclaim God's truth for you and me.

1

The Laborers in God's Vineyard: God Is Generous, and He Wants Us to Be Generous

Scripture: Matthew 20:1-16

Over and over again, Jesus liked to drive home a significant point by using the technique of contrast. Let me show you what I mean.

For example, in the parable of the prodigal son (Luke 15:11-32), the gracious love of the forgiving father is seen all the more powerfully as it is contrasted with the rigid, unbending bitterness of the elder brother.

In the parable of the Pharisee and the publican (Luke 18:9-14), the genuine humility of the publican is underscored more dramatically as it is set alongside the self-righteous arrogance of the proud Pharisee.

Also, the terrible plight of the poor man Lazarus (Luke 16:19-31) is shown even more graphically as his situation is compared to that of the indulgent, rich man who is commonly known as Dives.

In chapter 20 of Matthew we see it again, a fascinating contrast of personalities: the gracious and generous householder, over against the angry, resentful day laborers. But wait a minute; we are getting ahead of ourselves. The truth is that this parable is very perplexing and troublesome to many people, especially at first reading, and they (like the angry day laborers) cry out, "Unfair! Unfair!" Well, let's remember the parable together, and then let me give you a couple of keys that I think will unlock this story and enable us to learn the important truth Jesus intended to communicate through it.

The parable actually describes fairly well the kind of thing that happened each September in first-century Palestine. The grape harvest ripened toward the end of September, followed closely by the rainy season. It was urgent to get the grapes in before the rains came or else there would be extensive damage to the crop, and a big financial loss. More often than not, it was a frantic race against time. Any worker was welcome, even if he could give only an hour or so to the job.

Since this work was obviously seasonal, the householder did not have a regular crew of workers on hand to harvest the grapes. Rather, at just the right moment, he would go into the marketplace to find workers he could hire for the day to bring in the crop. In his commentary on Matthew, William Barclay describes it like this:

> The men who were standing in the marketplace were not street-corner idlers lazing away their time. In Palestine, the marketplace was the equivalent of the labor exchange. A man came there first thing in the morning, carrying his tools, and he waited until someone came and hired him. The men who stood in the marketplace were not gossiping idlers; they were waiting for work, and the fact that some of them stood on until even five o'clock in the evening is the proof of how desperately they wanted work. . . . With them, to be unemployed for a day was a disaster. (William Barclay, ed. *The Daily Study Bible; The Gospel of Matthew*, Vol. 2. Philadelphia: Westminster Press, 1975, pp. 245-46)

Now, the going rate for this kind of day labor was a *denarius.* That was not much money—about twenty cents in silver. Not much, but enough to buy food for your family for the night. Any less than that wouldn't do much good. Today, it would be like going grocery shopping with a dollar; you just can't feed your family for that. Why, I went to the supermarket the other day, got to the checkout counter, and discovered that I had bought $87 worth of stuff and still had nothing to eat! If a worker back then went home with less than a *denarius,* he would have a worried wife and hungry children. And the householder in this parable knew that!

The story begins as the householder senses that the harvesttime is at hand, and so he goes out early in the morning to hire workers. The workers agree to work for him that day for a *denarius* (the usual rate), and he sends them to the vineyard. Later that morning (about 9:00 A.M.) he realizes that more workers are needed. So he finds some more hands and sends them to work also, promising to pay them what is right. Twice more (at noon and at 3:00 P.M.) he does this. Throughout the day, he continues to put more and more workers in the vineyard to gather the grapes. It's getting more urgent now. The daylight hours are slipping away so quickly. It's urgent to get the crop in and get it in rapidly.

Still later, very late in the workday at "the eleventh hour," which means about 5:00 P.M., he gets desperate. Maybe he sees a cloud on the horizon; maybe it's a Friday and all work will soon have to stop for the Sabbath. Whatever the case, he knows that every second is precious now, every worker he can get is needed and time is a-wasting. So even at this late hour, he sends even more workers into the vineyard to help complete the harvest.

Finally, at the end of the day, he pays all the workers a full day's wage, a *denarius.* Those who had come early in the day are upset by this—irate, indignant, resentful. They march on the householder's house, chanting, "Unfair! Unfair!" And strangely at this point, the story reminds us of something we have heard before. Doesn't this sound like the elder brother in the parable of the prodigal son, who so bitterly resents his father's gracious treatment of the returning younger brother? He too shouts, "Unfair!" It's the same kind of situation, isn't it? "Unfair!" they cry.

But the householder responds to the workers who had been there from the beginning of the workday: "My friends, I did you no wrong. I paid you what we agreed upon. I gave you the fair going rate. Am I not allowed to be gracious to these others? I don't want their families to go hungry tonight. Do you? Do you really want to begrudge my generosity?"

Isn't this a great story? Perplexing at first; troublesome to many. But there are two significant keys here, two significant verses that unlock its great truth.

The first key is found in verse 1, indeed in the first seven words: "For the kingdom of heaven is like . . . " That's the clue. That's the key. You see, this story is not about labor relations, or fairness in the marketplace; it's about God and his kingdom! In this parable, Jesus is telling both his listeners and us that God's kingdom is not about laws and merit and earnings and privileges and benefits. No! It's about grace and acceptance and inclusiveness. It's about unconditional love. Whosoever will may come—even those who arrive late!

Now, let me bring this closer to home. Let me give you another hint: If you want to understand this parable better, just take it out of the setting of the vineyard, and apply it to the church. It means that those who join the church today are just as valid members, just as special, just as precious to God as those who joined forty years ago. And those who joined forty years ago will be the first ones to welcome them and accept them and include them, and to show them God's grace. "For the kingdom of heaven is like . . ." Those are the key words, because they remind us that this is not a story about today's workplace. It's a story about God and his kingdom, a story about God and his grace.

The second key that unlocks the story is in verse 15, where the householder says this: "Do you begrudge my generosity?" (RSV). Here is the point of the parable: God is gracious, kind, compassionate, and generous, and he wants us to be that way too. He wants us to imitate his caring, loving ways.

The Gospels make it clear: The people who get cut off from God are those who begrudge God's generosity. The elder brother in the parable of the prodigal son missed the party. Why? Because he begrudged his father's generosity. The religious leaders of the first century got aggravated and outdone with Jesus. Why? Because he spent so much time with the outcasts of society. They begrudged his generosity.

You know, we have misnamed this parable in Matthew 20:1-16. We call it the Parable of the

Laborers in the Vineyard, but Joachim Jeremias, who has written the classic book on the parables of Jesus, calls this story "The Parable of the Good Employer," and he is right. The star of this parable is God, not the laborers.

Now, what does this mean to you and me right now? What can we learn here for the practical living of these days? Perhaps this.

First of All, We See That There Is No Place in God's Kingdom for Resentment

When will we ever learn? Over and over again in the Gospels, Jesus warns us to beware of the resentful spirit. The workers in Matthew 20 are resentful and bitter over the good fortune of others, and bitterness and resentment like that just don't belong in God's kingdom. Frederick Buechner put it like this when he described the different kinds of love:

> The love for equals is a human thing . . . of friend for friend, brother for brother. It is to love what is loving and lovely. The world smiles.
>
> The love for the less fortunate is a beautiful thing . . . the love for those who suffer. . . . This is compassion, and it touches the heart of the world.

The love for the more fortunate is a rare thing . . . to love those who succeed where we fail, to rejoice without envy with those who rejoice. . . . The world is bewildered by its saints.

And then there is the love for the enemy . . . love for the one who does not love you but mocks, threatens, and inflicts pain. . . . This is God's love. It conquers the World.

(*The Magnificent Defeat*, New York: Seabury Press, p. 105)

It is *love* that is characteristic of God's kingdom—not resentment. There is no place in God's kingdom for resentment.

Second, There Is No Place in God's Kingdom for Selfishness

If the angry workers in Matthew 20 were upset about the kindness and generosity the householder was showing to the latecomers, they were even *more* concerned about the extra rewards and benefits they thought they should be getting themselves. That kind of selfishness is not a pretty picture.

One of Aesop's fables shows how costly selfishness can be. It's the story about a dog that is given a large, delicious bone by a neighbor one day. On his way home, the dog holds the bone firmly in his teeth while he crosses a bridge over a river. Looking down into the river, the dog sees his own reflection in the water, and he thinks it is another dog with a bone that is larger than the one given to him. He leans over and snaps at the dog that he sees in the river, and, of course, as he does, he drops the bone that he is carrying into the river below, and he goes home empty-handed and hungry.

That's what selfishness does to us, and that kind of greedy attitude has no place in God's kingdom.

Finally, There Is No Place in God's Kingdom for Arrogance

Arrogantly, the day laborers marched on the householder. They fussed at him, criticized him, berated him, challenged his goodness, and begrudged his generosity. That kind of self-righteous, haughty attitude doesn't fit in God's kingdom.

The world has been greatly inspired by the life and work and witness of the late Mother Teresa. Her ministry to the poor and dying in Calcutta is legendary. A clue to her greatness can be found in her daily prayer. It was her intense desire to live every day in the spirit of Jesus and to share his love and grace with everyone she met. That is expressed beautifully in her daily prayer:

> Dear Jesus, help me to spread Thy fragrance everywhere I go. Flood my soul with Thy spirit and love. Penetrate and possess my whole being so utterly that all my life may only be a radiance of Thine. Shine through me and be so in me that every soul I come in contact with may feel Thy presence in my soul. Let them look up and see no longer me but only Jesus. Stay with me and then I shall begin to shine as you shine, so to shine as to be a light to others.
>
> (From the video *Everyone, Everywhere*)*

That's what this parable is all about—the gracious, unconditional love of God—and the point for us is clear: God is generous and kind to us, and he wants us to be generous and kind to one another. And to everyone we meet!

Everyone, Everywhere is a film by Miles O'Brien Riley, based on the life and work of Mother Teresa in Calcutta. Produced by Franciscan Communications. Copyright © 1996-2004 St. Anthony Messenger Press.

2
The Pharisee and the Publican: Plugging into the Power Source

Scripture: Luke 18:9-14

Some years ago, when I went off to seminary, I won some scholarships. The scholarships helped a lot with my school expenses, but the money was not nearly enough to pay for tuition, books, fees, food, and room and board. So, I had to work. In addition to being a full-time theological student, I pastored two churches and I was a janitor on the seminary campus.

It was in the janitorial job that I met a wonderful man, Mr. Johnson. He was in his late seventies at the time, and he was my immediate supervisor. Three first-year students were assigned to work under Mr. Johnson in the care and cleaning of a large building on campus. None of us students knew anything about janitorial work, and the truth is we were all in our early twenties, so we weren't that interested. We had all kinds of ideas about the Bible and theology and sports and fast food, but we were real rookies when it came to the care and maintenance of buildings. Mr. Johnson decided to teach us, and he taught us a lot. Actually, we found out later that there is a lot more of that kind of work involved in being a pastor than we realized. With genuine respect, Mr. Johnson called each of us "Mister," but when he wanted to give us a lesson, he would always say, "Boys, what do you see?" That meant he saw something that needed fixing, and more often than not, we didn't see anything. Then, Mr. Johnson would point out the problem, such as a smudge on the window, a spot on the wall, or a stain on the floor, and he would say, "Boys, you can't fix the problem if you can't see the problem."

One morning I was assigned to wax and buff the floor in one of the main classrooms. I got down on my hands and knees and applied the wax, but when I got ready to buff the floor, the electric buffer would not turn on. It wouldn't do anything. Just then, Mr. Johnson walked by and saw that I was having a problem. "Mr. Moore," he said, "what do you see?" "I see that the buffer won't come on," I said. And then Mr. Johnson smiled and said, "Mr. Moore, I have been doing this kind of work for a long time now, and over my long years of experience I have learned that the electric buffer works best when it is plugged into the power source!" Then he walked over, plugged the buffer into the electrical outlet, and of course it started right up.

This is an appropriate parable for many people today, isn't it? God's power is available. God's strength is accessible. God's energy is at hand. God's presence is nearer than breathing. God's forgiveness is freely offered. But some lives just are not connected! They live in the shadow of the power source, but they are not plugged in!

We see this dramatically in Jesus' parable of the Pharisee and the publican. Evidently the publican, this tax collector, had had a bad day, maybe one of the worst days of his life, because he was driven by his problems to the Temple, ashamed, groping, sorrowful, remorseful, beating upon his chest.

Catch the agony of that now: "beating upon his chest"—the vivid, dramatic, heart-wrenching symbol of penitence. Jesus tells us that this man, this painfully penitent man, went home *justified*, rather than the other man. The publican's worst day may have turned out to be his best day, because his worst day brought him back to God. It caused him to plug in to the power of God's grace. While the other, the Pharisee, lived daily in the presence of God (he was a religious professional), somehow he was not connected; he was not plugged into the power source. Remember the story with me.

This story is found only in the Gospel of Luke, and that is fitting because in Luke's Gospel, we see over and over how much Jesus loved stories with surprise endings, and how much he loved stories where in the end the little guy comes out on top. We see both of those elements in this great parable.

Two men go up to the Temple to pray. One is a Pharisee, and the other is a publican, a tax collector. The Pharisee, the symbol of religious authority in that day, marches proudly in. This is his turf. He is a big man at the Temple. He knows his way around, and he strides in. Using his most arrogant swagger, he marches to the most prominent spot in that sacred place to show off how pious he is. *People will be very impressed with my religiosity, and well they should,* he reasons, and then he prays this prayer: "God, I thank you that I am not like other people: thieves, rogues, adulterers, or even like this tax collector. I fast twice a week [by the way, the law demanded only one fast per week]; I give a tenth of all my income" (Luke 18:11-12). (The law required that only agricultural products be tithed.) So prays the proud Pharisee. But the tax collector, in humility and penitence, stands reverently toward the back of the Temple, far from the altar. He beats upon his chest, ashamed of what he has done. He plugs into the power of God's grace, and he prays for forgiveness: "God, be merciful to me, a sinner!" (v. 13).

Jesus concludes the parable by saying, "I tell you, this man [the humble, penitent tax collector, this man who plugged into the power of God's mercy] went down to his home justified rather than the other" (v. 14), the arrogant Pharisee who relied upon and bragged about his own religious accomplishments. And then Jesus concludes with this statement: "All who exalt themselves will be humbled, but all who humble themselves will be exalted."

It's a great story, isn't it? There's so much here to think about, but for now let's focus on what we can learn from the Pharisee's failure. Somehow, he was not connected, not plugged in. Let me lift up three thoughts about this. I'm sure you will think of others.

First of All, the Pharisee Was Not Plugged into Gratitude

The Pharisee started his prayer with the words "God, I thank you," and that sounds good; it sounds like the beginning of a prayer of thanksgiving. But as we read on, we realize that his prayer is not really one of humble gratitude, but rather one of haughty self-congratulation.

Entertainment personality Art Linkletter once asked a little girl named Debbie, who was studying general science, "What is salt?" And Debbie answered, "Salt is what spoils the potatoes when you leave it out." We might ask, "What is gratitude?" and answer with little Debbie that gratitude is what spoils a gift when it is left out.

Some years ago when William Stidger was a professor at the School of Theology in Boston, shortly before Thanksgiving one November, he began to think of all the blessings he had in life. He thought of special people who over the years had helped him, encouraged him, and inspired him. He remembered a schoolteacher who had done so much for him. She had put deep within him a love for poetry. So, William Stidger sat down and wrote a letter of thanks to his former schoolteacher. Her reply touched him deeply. Here is what she said:

My Dear Willie,

I cannot tell you how much your note meant to me. I am in my eighties, living alone in a small room, cooking my own meals, lonely and, like the last leaf of autumn, lingering behind. You will be interested to know that I taught school for fifty years and yours is the first note of appreciation I ever received. It came on a blue-cold morning, and it cheered me as nothing has in many years.

William Stidger wept over that note. He thought then of other people who had been kind to him. He remembered one of his bishops who had been most helpful to him way back at the beginning of his ministry. The bishop was in retirement and had recently lost his wife. Dr. Stidger sat down again and wrote a belated letter of thanks to his former bishop. Back came this response:

My Dear Will:

Your letter was so beautiful, so real, that as I sat reading it in my study, tears fell from my eyes, tears of gratitude. Then, before I realized what I was doing, I rose from my chair and called her name to share it with her, forgetting—for a moment—she was gone. You will never know how much your letter has warmed my spirit. I have been walking around in the glow of it all day long.

(W. E. Sangster, *Sangster's Special Day Sermons* [Nashville: Abingdon Press, 1960] pp. 147-48).

Now, let me tell you something. Nice as it is to receive gratitude, it is even better to give it. Nice as it is to hear a word of thanks, it is even better to express it. The truth is, the closer we get to God, the more grateful we become.

Well, how is it with you right now? Are you plugged into gratitude? Are you a grateful person? Is it natural for you to express appreciation? Is it easy for you to say thanks to others and to God?

The Pharisee came up short that day because he was not plugged into the spirit of thanksgiving. He couldn't appreciate anything because he was so caught up in himself, his own credentials, his own accomplishments, his own self-interest, and his own vain religiosity. He missed the boat that day because he was not connected to the spirit of gratitude. Please don't let that happen to you, because life works better and faith works better when we are plugged into gratitude.

Second, He Was Not Plugged Into Generosity

When will we ever learn? The Pharisee tried to make himself look good by trashing the tax collector, and it boomeranged on him. That's the way it works. We bash other people, and it comes back to haunt us. We try to make ourselves look good by making other people look bad, and in the very process of "looking down our noses" at other people, we are the ones who get smudged. We reveal far more about ourselves than we reveal about the one we are criticizing or condemning.

You may have heard the story about a man who was walking through a large shopping mall one Saturday morning. He noticed a little boy walking along by himself, looking in the windows. The little boy seemed happy and carefree, but he appeared to be unattended, and he was so young and so small to be in that huge mall all alone. The man was making his way over to check on the little boy when all of a sudden a voice blared out over the public address system: "Will Christopher Walker please come to the big clock in the center of the mall? Christopher Walker, please come to the big clock in the center of the mall." Just then, the man heard the little boy mumble to himself, "Oh rats! I'm lost again!" Evidently, little Christopher had wandered off before.

That can happen to us in our faith pilgrimage: We can get lost. Every time we wander away from the spirit of love, every time we wander away from the spirit of kindness, every time we wander away from the spirit of graciousness, every time we wander away from the spirit of generosity, we are lost, because we have lost the spirit of Christ.

If somehow Jesus Christ could walk into this parable of the Pharisee and the tax collector, if Jesus had walked into the Temple that day, what would he have done? He would not have looked down his nose at the anguished tax collector. He would not have sneered at him, criticized him, condemned him, or pointed at him in derision. No! Jesus would have felt his pain, and he would have gone over and put his arms around the shoulders of that penitent and distraught man, and he would have said to him, "How can I help you?" And that's the way Jesus wants us to be—loving, caring, kind, and generous. He wants us to live in that spirit. He gave his love for us on the cross, and now he wants us not to bash and trash other people, but rather to pass his healing love on to them, to share his redemptive love with them.

You see, the closer we get to God, the more grateful we are, and the more generous we are. The Pharisee missed out that day because somehow he had wandered off. He was not plugged into gratitude or generosity.

Third and Finally, He Was Not Plugged into God

Fred Craddock is one of the great preachers of our time. He tells about a young minister just out of seminary, just starting out in his ministry, wanting to do well, but scared to death. The first time the young minister went to the hospital to make his first round of pastoral calls, he was pretty nervous and felt anxious and inadequate. "O God, be with me," he muttered softly as he walked through the front door of the hospital.

The young minister made a couple of visits that were relatively routine, and all went smoothly. But then as he entered the next room, he saw an elderly woman lying on the bed, gravely ill, gasping for breath. The minister decided fairly quickly to make this a short visit, so he said to her, "I can see you're having a hard day, so I won't stay, but could I have a quick prayer with you?" "Oh yes, please," answered the woman. "I want you to pray that I will be made well, that God will give me my health."

That really shook the young minister up. He gulped, but he prayed the best he could. When the prayer ended, the older woman's eyes flashed open. Immediately she sat up. She startled the young preacher by throwing her legs over the side of the bed. She stood up. She stretched out her arms. She turned toward the young minister and said, "I feel better. I think I've been healed!" Then she walked straight out of that room and skipped joyfully down to the nurses' station, shouting, "Look at me! Look at me! I think I am healed!"

The young minister staggered out of the room, went down the stairs, out the door of the hospital, and into the parking lot. As he stood at his car, before opening the door, he looked up and said, "Oh Lord, don't you ever do that to me again!" That young minister wanted to be close to God, but not that close! (From Fred Craddock, Newnham Lecturer, First United Methodist Church, Longview, Texas, 1988).

That was the Pharisee's problem too, wasn't it? He wanted God in his life, but not too close. He wanted to be connected to God, but not too tightly. He wanted to be plugged into God, but not too personally. Really, he wanted to hold God at arm's length. He wanted to rely on his own efforts, brag about his own accomplishments, toot his own horn. He was operating on the false assumption that we can earn God's forgiveness. But look at how off-target he was. God forgives us, not because we are good, but because God is good; not because we are great, but because God is great; not because of any good works we do, but because of the gracious saving work God did for us on an "old rugged cross."

The Pharisee came to the Temple that day, but he was not plugged in—not plugged into gratitude or to generosity or to God. And arrogantly, self-righteously, he shouted, "Look at me! How good I am!" On the other hand, the tax collector came in humility that day, and in his anguish, he said the prayer of penitence, a prayer we all need to pray: "God, be merciful to me, a sinner. Come into my life as never before, and by your amazing grace, heal me, save me, redeem me, forgive me."

3

The Weeds Among the Wheat: Watch Those Overreactions!

Scripture: Matthew 13:24-30

Much of the misery in the world today is caused by hasty, explosive overreactions. Friendships are destroyed, marriages are disrupted, churches are split, wars are started, lives are lost, and hearts are broken, all due to impulsive overreaction. A problem presents itself, and then someone facing that problem overreacts to the point that the "overcorrection" is worse than the original problem.

Let me illustrate this with a few life vignettes.

Some months ago, a woman in our church was driving alone down a country road. As she came out of a curve heading toward a narrow bridge, she drove into a nightmare experience that only a great faith and tenacious determination enabled her to survive. As she rounded the curve, her right front wheel struck a bad place in the road, forcing the car over onto the right shoulder and out of control.

Frightened (as anyone would have been), she jerked the steering wheel hard to the left, but too strongly. She overcorrected, and the car swerved back all the way across the road, sideswiped the end of the bridge, and catapulted eighty feet through the air into the creek, landing with the front wheels on the opposite bank and the rest of the car submerged in the water.

With water up to her shoulders, a broken arm, broken ribs, a fractured neck, facial cuts, and crushed legs, she struggled to keep her head above water. She waited for what must have seemed like an eternity and prayed with all her might. An hour later, help finally arrived. Let me hurry to tell you that she not only survived that terrible ordeal, but in so doing she became a great inspiration to all who know her.

Isn't that an interesting parable for life? It is so easy when we are under pressure to overcorrect, to overreact, and sometimes the real dangers are in the overreaction.

I recently read about a Methodist Sunday school teacher who taught the third-grade class. In her class, the teacher had twin girls who seemed quite happy and never missed church or Sunday school. The twins came from a poor family, and their dresses were worn and out of style, but it didn't seem to bother them because every Sunday they were right there at the Methodist church. But the Sunday school teacher, concerned about the twins, took up some money and bought the girls some beautiful new dresses.

The very next Sunday however, the twin girls were missing. They didn't show up for Sunday school. The teacher, alarmed, called their home immediately to see if they were sick. "Oh, no, they are not sick," explained the mother. "They just looked so nice in their new dresses that I sent them to the Presbyterian church!" Sometimes our overcorrection can come back to haunt us.

We all should know this point well. We have seen it in old western movies a hundred times. A man suspected of wrongdoing is put in jail to await trial. The judge has to come over from Dodge City, a three-day journey. But some of the townspeople can't wait. They want their town purged of evil right now, even though the evidence against the man is not conclusive.

They quickly condemn the man, organize a lynch mob, and march to the jail with torches and a rope to "string up" the suspect. But the sheriff holds them off. He tells them they can't do this; they can't take the law in their own hands; they can't condemn this man to death without a fair trial; they have no real conclusive evidence on this man, and no right to kill him.

The sheriff says, "Be patient! Trust the courts! Wait for the trial! Only the judge has the right to determine whether or not the suspect is guilty. Be patient! Don't go overboard! Justice will be served, and righteousness will prevail." Of course, you remember from those old western movies that most every time, it turned out that the mob was wrong and the suspect was innocent, and the townspeople were embarrassed by their hasty, explosive overreaction.

One of the Kingdom parables of Jesus in Matthew's Gospel makes the point. It underscores the danger of overreaction. It is traditionally called the Parable of the Wheat and the Tares, or the Parable of the Weeds Among the Wheat. In this parable, Jesus is calling for patience, and warning us against hasty, emotional, impulsive, violent action. Be patient!

Trust God! Trust the test of time! The truth will come out!

Remember how it goes. Jesus said that the kingdom of heaven is like a man who had sown his field with wheat. He had been very particular about the good quality of the seed. But during the night, the man's enemy came and sowed weeds among the wheat, then slipped away into the darkness. Later the servants went out into the field, where they expected to find a good grain crop. But to their amazement and dismay, they found weeds growing among the wheat! The servants came back and asked the master: "Sir, did you not sow good seed? Where did the weeds come from?" He answered: "An enemy has done this!"

The servants, filled with anger, impulsively wanted to act immediately, explosively, and violently. They wanted to purge the field. They wanted to go out and rip up the weeds and get rid of them right away. But the master was a man of patience and self-control. He said: "No! Let's wait, for if you pull up the weeds now, you might harm the wheat. We will wait and let both grow together, and then I will separate them at the harvest. Then we will get rid of the weeds and gather the wheat into my barn."

Now, there are several interesting observations that can be made from this fascinating parable. Let me list some of them.

1. For one thing, the parable reminds us that there are no perfect situations; there are always weeds among the wheat.

2. The parable also makes it clear that the Master is not responsible for the weeds. He sowed only the best seed, but somehow we have cultivated weeds rather than the Bread of Life.

3. The parable also underscores the fact that there are some judgments we are not capable of making. They belong to the Master.

4. And it shows that the weeds and wheat may look alike at first, but they are ultimately distinguished by their fruits.

5. And there is good news here: There will be a harvest. The weeds will not choke out the wheat, so be patient, keep your balance, sow good seed, and trust God to bring it out right.

Now, all of these observations are important. In fact, each one is a sermon in itself. But for now, I want to zero in on another element in this parable, the point we have already underscored: the dangers of overreacting! Jesus is giving a clear warning here. Don't overreact! Don't overcorrect! Be patient! Give it time! Keep your balance! Overreactions can be dangerous and destructive! Let me show you what I mean by bringing this closer to home.

First of All, Overreaction Can Be Dangerous Because It May Cause You to Lose Your Temper

Have you ever heard someone say something like this: "Oh, everybody knows I was born with a hot temper, but my temper is like a cyclone. It blows up quickly and just as quickly blows away." What people who overreact and lose their temper don't realize is this: Their temper may rise quickly like a cyclone, it may pass quickly like a cyclone, but also like a cyclone, it leaves behind immeasurable hurt, agony, heartache, and devastation.

In my opinion, loss of temper is always overreaction. I cannot remember a single time in my life when I lost my temper and later felt good about it. Always in my experience, loss of temper has been followed by remorse and guilt and shame. Now, let me hurry to say that I'm not talking about righteous indignation. There are some things happening in our world today that ought to make us angry. I'm not talking about that. I'm talking about just what the phrase says: losing it, losing your temper.

Some years ago, when our daughter, Jodi, was a baby, just a few months old at the time, my wife, June, went off to shop one Saturday morning and left me home to be the babysitter. It was the first time I had kept our new daughter all by myself. I put her on the floor in one of those plastic infant seats and started reading. (Now, let me digress to say that I had already decided that my daughter was not going to ever fall down or get hurt in any way. I was going to always be there to see that she was provided for and protected.) But I got so interested in the book I was reading that I didn't notice her leaning up out of that infant seat, rocking forward. All of a sudden, she toppled out of the infant seat face forward onto the carpet, screaming and crying at the top of her voice. I was startled, frightened, worried, frustrated, scared, and mad at myself. I threw my book aside, and in my haste to correct the situation I ran right over and accidentally stepped on her hand, and that hurt her worse than the fall; it hurt me worse, too!

Temper is like that, isn't it? It is an overreaction that erupts out of frustrating fear, guilt, and unhappiness with yourself, and it always makes matters worse; it hurts everybody involved. Let a Scout leader lose his temper one time, or let a minister lose his temper one time, and it is once too often. Overreaction is dangerous because it can cause you to lose your temper.

Second, Overreaction Can Cause You to Lose Your Marriage

Many divorces come about because one or both parties overreacted. In the counseling room, I often suggest to couples that there is a significant difference between "reacting" and "responding." You can react, or you can respond.

For example, the wife might say to her husband, "I wish we had more time together." Now, he has a choice. He can react and get defensive and say, "Oh, no! Here we go again. Nag, nag, nag, that's all I ever hear! I'm working my fingers to the bone for our family, and all I get are complaints. Why doesn't she grow up?" Now, you see, that's a *reaction*, a negative reaction, an overreaction. But, he doesn't have to react; rather, he can respond. When his wife says, "I wish we had more time together," he can react negatively and regard it as nagging, or he can respond positively by hearing it like this: *Hey! She loves me! She wants to be with me. She wants us to be together. Isn't that wonderful? Well, let's see what we can do about it.*

You see, the choice is yours. You can react to each other or you can respond. But if you react too often, too much, too violently, you may lose your marriage. Making a marriage work today takes a lot of patience, a lot of trust, a lot of working, a lot of listening, a lot of love, and a lot of responding.

Third, Overreaction Can Cause You to Lose Your Church

Some years ago, I saw a study on why people drop out of church. It had some interesting ideas. For example, the study suggested that only about one-half of all church members are real dropout candidates, and these are persons who handle stress less well and tend to run when it appears.

Second, these persons drop out because some problem arises, and it is almost always a misunderstanding, a small problem toward which the person is overreacting.

Third, dropouts either will blame others for the problem or will turn it within and blame themselves.

And fourth, deep down inside the dropouts suspect they may be overreacting, so they "sit in the window" for awhile—in other words, they stop going to church to see if anyone notices their absence, hoping someone will notice and invite them back. If no one notices, the problem is confirmed as a big one. They then will go out and reorganize their activities around something else. (Adapted from a dissertation by Dr. John Savage, a United Methodist minister in New York State; used by his permission.)

Let me say something to you with all the feeling I have in my heart. Please don't let that happen to you. Don't get your feelings hurt. Don't feel neglected. Don't let some little problem that really doesn't matter ruin your life. Don't overreact and lose your church. If you are here, stay here. If you've dropped out, then come on back. Or if you've never been in the church, there's no better time than now. Overreaction is dangerous because it can cause you to lose your temper, your marriage, and your church.

Overreaction Can Cause You to Lose Your Spiritual Balance

There are two sides to this coin, this state of balance, aren't there?

On the one hand, there is the young man brought up in a conservative home, who gets away on his own for the first time and over-reacts to his new freedom and thinks, *Anything goes. I can do anything I want to do.* That is not freedom, and you can only hope that he gets his balance before he ruins his life.

On the other side of the coin, there are persons who have a religious experience, who "get religion" and then overreact to the point where they want to force their experience on everybody they meet. The result is that they drive people away. Their overreaction prevents them from doing what they want most. They want to share their faith, but they come on so strongly that they drive people away.

Some years ago, our niece Leslie, who was two-and-a-half years old, got lost in the woods for over three hours in Winston-Salem, North Carolina. The sheriff's patrol, three volunteer fire departments, neighbors, and bloodhounds all stormed into the woods. This commotion scared Leslie, and she hid from them. They came on so strongly, she hid from them, grew tired, and fell asleep.

Finally, two little playmates said they thought they could find her, so the authorities pulled everybody back to a reasonable (though still fairly close) distance. The two little girls went into the woods, and in less than five minutes they had found Leslie and brought her out—tired, confused, a little scared, and very dusty, but safe and sound.

Sometimes in the name of religion people charge in so strongly that they scare others off. I once heard a woman describe her husband like this. She said, "He has become so pious, so arrogant, so 'holier than thou,' that now even when he says something right, he says it in such a way that it makes everybody else want to be wrong!" Think of it like this:

If we could be proud without being prideful;
reverent without being pompous;
bright without being snobbish;
serious without being sad;
concerned without being a crackpot;
committed without being closed-minded;
pure without being prudish; and
good without being "holier than thou,"
then our souls could be whole and healthy
and vibrant.

This is the message Jesus was giving us in the parable of the weeds among the wheat: Keep your balance! Don't overcorrect! Be patient!

Watch those overreactions! Rudyard Kipling, in his poem entitled "If", put it like this:

If you can keep your head when all about you
Are losing theirs and blaming it on you;
If you can trust yourself when all men doubt you,
But make allowance for their doubting too;
If you can wait and not be tired by waiting,
Or being lied about, don't deal in lies,
Or being hated, don't give way to hating.
And yet don't look too good, nor talk too wise;

If you can dream—and not make dreams your master;
If you can think—and not make thoughts your aim;
If you can meet with triumph and disaster
And treat those two impostors just the same;
If you can bear to hear the truth you've spoken
Twisted by knaves to make a trap for fools,
Or watch the things you gave your life to broken,
And stoop and build 'em up with worn-out tools;

If you can make one heap of all your win-
nings
And risk it on one turn of pitch-and-toss,
And lose, and start again at your begin-
nings
And never breathe a word about your loss;
If you can force your heart and nerve and
sinew
To serve your turn long after they are gone,
And so hold on when there is nothing in
you
Except the Will which says to them: "Hold
on;"

If you can talk with crowds and keep your
virtue,
Or walk with kings—nor lose the common
touch
If neither foes nor loving friends can hurt
you;
If all men count with you, but none too
much
If you can fill the unforgiving minute
With sixty seconds' worth of distance
run—
Yours is the Earth and everything that's in
it,
And—what is more—you'll be a Man, my
son!

What a great poem this is, and what a great parable this is in Matthew 13, the Parable of the Weeds Among the Wheat. In both the poem and the parable, we are reminded not to over-react, but rather to be patient. Jesus is reminding us in this parable always to do our best and then trust God for the rest.

4
The Ten Pounds:
Use It or Lose It

Scripture: Luke 19:11-26

The telephone rang loudly in a police station in New York City. The sergeant at the precinct desk handled the call with dispatch. He knew exactly what to do. He had handled this kind of call many times before. It was routine now—almost commonplace. Another drunk was lying unconscious in a street gutter in the Bowery.

Quickly, the police and the emergency squad responded. They were on the scene promptly, sirens blaring, lights flashing. They did their best to revive the man, but it was too late. He had breathed his last. Some of the curious onlookers who were familiar with the people and the happenings in the Bowery recognized the dead man in the gutter. He was a well-known character in that section of the city. He went about every day selling shoestrings and cigarette butts for drinks. He was in his late forties, but he looked at least seventy because of the kind of life he had been leading. In a sense, he had unconsciously committed suicide, drowning himself in a relentless sea of alcoholic drinks. Another Bowery drunk had died, they said. "What's so unusual about that? It's a common enough occurrence. It happens all the time."

But let me tell you more of this tragic story. When the authorities reached the city morgue with the body, they found in his pockets a few coins, a few shoestrings, a few cigarette butts, some identification papers, and, oh yes, one other thing: they found a Phi Beta Kappa key!

Further investigation revealed that the man had been brought up in a fine home and had graduated from Harvard University with a perfect 4.0 academic record! What had happened? Wouldn't you like to know the rest of that story? I'm sorry I don't know more. However, out of what we do know of the story, one thing is clear: Though that man died that day in a street gutter in the Bowery, the truth is that he had quit on life a long time before that moment of physical death. Spiritually and emotionally, he had died long before.

Psychologists tell us that as long as we live, we have two desires working within us, doing battle against each other. One is the desire to give up, to pull back, to throw in the towel and quit on life. The other is the desire to move forward through struggle and effort, stretching and growing, striving and celebrating life. Of course, the call of the Christian is to move forward and embrace life. But, sadly, far too many people (like the man in the Bowery, although less dramatically) give up and give in to the desire to quit on life. They start out well with starry eyes, great fervor, ready to conquer the world and live life to the full; but then come problems, difficulties, responsibilities, nuisances, burdens, troubles, disappointments, heartaches, and disillusionment. Suddenly, they feel hoodwinked and deceived. They feel persecuted and put upon. They feel cheated. They feel that life has dealt them a poor hand, a hand not nearly so favorable as that which others are holding. So they fold up their tent and give up. No longer do they really live. They pull back into a hard shell. Life for them becomes merely a series of escapes. They cope, they exist, they vegetate, they get by, but in essence they have frozen up and quit on life.

Jesus once told a parable about this kind of quiet tragedy. We call it the Parable of the Talents in Matthew, and the Parable of the Ten Pounds in Luke. A more contemporary name might be the Parable of Investments. Remember the story with me. Once there was a nobleman who went on a long journey. Before he left he called in three of his servants and gave them a pound each. Now, in that time, a pound represented about 100 days' wages, so it was a significant amount of money given to each. The man told his servants to invest his money and see how much they could make while he was gone.

When he returned, he called the servants in to see how they had done. The first two servants had invested their money wisely and had done quite well, and they were commended for a job well done. But the third servant had been afraid, afraid to even try. He had done nothing but hide the money in a piece of cloth. His lack of imagination and his lack of effort cost him dearly. Not only did he miss out on a promotion, but he lost all the money and his position as well.

Now, what is this story all about? Of course, I know that a parable is a story designed to underscore one central point, but if I may use poetic and theological license, I would like to point out that there are several fascinating and important insights here. For example, the parable shows us that mere abstinence from evil is not enough; we must use our gifts to do good. The parable also shows us dramatically that if we don't use our gifts and talents, we lose them. Ask any musician or athlete about that. They know how true that is, "Use it or lose it." The parable also illustrates how life is a sacred trust, and somehow we are accountable to God for it.

Of course, all of these insights are important. We could write volumes on each one of them. But what I want to look at more closely is the question of why the third servant failed. What immobilized him? What paralyzed him? What went wrong? Well, he failed because he did nothing. He failed because he froze. Now, that still happens, doesn't it? We talk about being scared stiff, scared to death, numb with fear. In the theater, we call it stage fright. In athletics, we call it choking. It can also happen spiritually, but how? That's the question: What causes us to freeze up in our faith pilgrimage?

First, We Can Be Frozen by Our Appetites

Dr. Harry Emerson Fosdick, when he was pastor of the Riverside Church in New York City, told a fascinating story about a vulture who was frozen and ultimately destroyed by his own appetites. It was a wintry day on the Niagara River near Buffalo, New York. This vulture (a bird of prey) had alighted on a carcass floating down the river, and he began to feed. He intended to feed on the carcass as long as he could, and then to depart just before the rapids broke. He planned to feed right up to the last second, until just before the falls, and then break away and fly to safety into the skies. But something happened that the vulture hadn't counted on. Moving swiftly toward the dangerous waterfalls, the vulture tried to fly away and escape, but he couldn't! He could not get away because on that cold, wintry day, his claws had frozen to the carcass he was feeding upon, and he was plunged over the falls to his death! He meant to break free at the last moment, but his talons were frozen. He was imprisoned and destroyed by the clutch of his own claws! Our hands freeze to that which we feed on.

Some time ago in Houston a poignant thing happened. A young man broke into a convenience store, and then once inside he called the police and asked them to come and arrest him. Why would he do that? Because he was addicted to crack cocaine. He had a $3,000-a-week drug habit. He knew he had a big problem that was paralyzing him, a problem he could not handle alone, and he said that was the only way he knew to get help. We can be frozen and immobilized and destroyed by our appetites.

The truth is that many people today are indeed slaves to their appetites; they let one thing take control of their lives and immobilize them. Prejudice, envy, a bad temper, revenge, worry, drugs, possessions, guilt—if we feed on things like that, we can be frozen in our tracks by our appetites.

How is it with you? Is there one thing in your life that is enslaving you? The point is clear. We can be frozen by our appetites.

Second, We Can Be Frozen by Our Attitudes

Dr. Leonard Sweet, author and professor of evangelism at Drew Theological Seminary, tells about a woman who was a member of a church he served some years ago. Her name was Wilma. Dr. Sweet said that Wilma had the worst attitude he had ever encountered, always sullen, somber, cynical, sour, bitter, pessimistic. She was angry at life, against everything, and critical of everybody. Dr. Sweet wondered why. He looked into it and discovered that Wilma had not always been like that. To the contrary, just a few years before, she had been quite the opposite—bright, happy, positive, energetic, optimistic. Dr. Sweet discovered that five years earlier, a drunk driver had run his car up onto the sidewalk and hit Wilma's two-year-old daughter, Kristi. Kristi was killed instantly, and Wilma was devastated. In her grief, someone who meant well had said a terrible thing to Wilma. Trying to explain Kristi's death, someone said, "Wilma, every now and then God gets tired of stale, worn-out flowers, and he wants a fresh young rosebud for his bouquet."

Dr. Sweet said that when he heard that, he understood why Wilma was bitter and sullen, sad and cynical, and he was able to say to her, "Wilma, don't you believe that for another minute. It was not God's will for your two-year-old daughter to die. It was not God's will that Kristi should be hit by a car. It happened because a man made a bad decision, and he tried to drive while he was drunk. That's what

did it, not God. God's heart was broken too."
(Personal story from Dr. Leonard Sweet, told by
him in a sermon given at a workshop at the
Upper Room, Nashville; used with Dr. Sweet's
permission.)

Somehow that conversation with Dr. Sweet
touched a chord deep down in Wilma's soul. It
thawed her frozen heart, and her attitudes
changed. She wasn't mad at God anymore. She
wasn't angry at life anymore. Slowly but surely
she was able to move forward with her life,
and she became a positive, productive, loving
person again.

Here's the point: Our theology affects our
attitudes! How we feel about God greatly
affects how we feel about life. Jesus talked a lot
about attitudes. The inner life was very important to him, and that's why he said over and
over things like this: "Don't be afraid! Don't be
anxious! God loves you. God will always be
with you. You can count on that. God is on
your side!"

Now, if you hear that, really hear that, and
believe that, it will change your attitudes and
change your life. It will make you a happier,
more confident person. It will make you more
productive and more optimistic. But this parable has a strong warning for us. Namely, that

we can be frozen by our destructive appetites and by our attitudes.

Finally, We Can Be Frozen Too by Our Anxieties

In the parable, the third servant didn't try because he was afraid, afraid to act. His fears immobilized him.

There is a story about a man who went to the doctor because he was tired and run-down all the time. The doctor checked him over and then said, "The best thing you can do is stop drinking, go on a diet, start jogging, stop carousing around town every night! That's the best thing you can do." The man was thoughtful for a moment and then asked, "What's the *next* best thing?"

Isn't that the way most of us are? We feel ourselves getting caught in a trap and we want to break free, but we are afraid to pay the price, afraid to act, afraid to even try. There are people today who know there is something they ought to do, but like the third servant, they are afraid to act, afraid to try, afraid to commit.

I'm thinking of the father who knows he needs to spend more time with his children, but somehow he never gets around to it.

I'm thinking of the person who has a broken relationship, is estranged from another person. He knows it ought to be set right, but he is afraid to try.

I'm thinking of that married couple who know that communication is breaking down in their marriage, but they just let it go and continue to drift apart.

I'm thinking of those persons who ought to come on and join the church, but they continue to put it off.

I'm thinking of those people who have dropped out of the church, who know they need to come back, but somehow they are afraid, afraid to act, and they are all imprisoned and frozen by their fears.

What's the answer? How do we get thawed out and set free? Christ sets us free by showing us that love casts out fear! Alan Walker graphically makes this point in the following story:

> Here is an incident [that] illustrates the power of love. It happened at Marburg in Germany. A mother was at a circus with a little girl who suddenly slipped out of her sight and disappeared. The next moment her mother saw that the child had pressed through the bars of the lion's cage in the circus. There she was, next to

the lion in the cage. The lion already had its claws near the child. The mother, without a moment's hesitation, rushed in the door of the cage and threw it open. She went into the lion's cage, she grasped the child in her arms, brought her out, slammed the door of the cage in the lion's face, and fainted.

Now, that woman feared a lion as much as you and I do, but for the moment love cast out fear.

(Alan Walker, *Jesus the Liberator* [Nashville: Abingdon Press, 1973] p. 22.)

The little girl's mother did a risky, dangerous thing that she would have thought impossible for her to do, out of her love for her endangered child. The point is obvious: Love is the freeing agent. Love is the thawing agent. When love is strong enough, you can be sure it will cast out fear and bring you out of whatever imprisons you. You see, love sets us free from destructive appetites, from negative attitudes, and from crippling anxieties, and love lets us be God's children and God's stewards in the world.

5

Dives and Lazarus:
The One Thing More Costly
Than Caring Is Not Caring

Scripture: Luke 16:10-31

There is only one thing more costly than caring, and that is not caring! Without question, love for others is indeed demanding, but the alternatives are deadly. I am sure that nothing pleases God more than to see us actively and tenderly caring for one another. I am equally sure that when God sees us being selfish, calloused, cruel, unfeeling, and uncaring, it must break God's heart.

Please notice something in the scriptures that is highly significant. Don't miss this, now:

The Bible makes it very clear that we are all accountable to God! We may (for a time) ignore that or forget that or try to wish it away, but ultimately we all have to answer to God. We all have to stand before God and answer for our lives. And, interestingly, the teachings of Jesus remind us over and over again that one of the key judgment questions will be simply this: How did you treat your neighbor? How did you treat other people? That's the question God has for us.

Let me document this. For example, we see it in the parable of the last judgment in Matthew 25 (vv. 31-46). Some of the people are on one side, and some are on the other. Some receive a great blessing, and some miss out. Why? The distance between them is not really so great, but their destinies are poles apart. Jesus explains here that the difference in destinies is caused by, what? Little acts of love, little acts of charity, little acts of caring—a sandwich for a hungry man, clothes to a needy person, a cup of water to one who is thirsty, a kindness to a stranger, a visit to someone sick or in prison. That was all, just those little acts of self-giving! The way we handle those opportunities for caring makes all the difference in where we come out.

We see it again in the parable of the good Samaritan (Luke 10:25-37). The Samaritan is called good for one reason and one reason only—because he cared enough to act, because he cared enough to help, because he cared enough to do something good for someone in need. Notice also, in the parable of the prodigal son (Luke 15:11-32), that it is the elder brother's unwillingness to love his brother that keeps him out of his father's party.

How did you treat your neighbor; how did you treat other people? That is the question we are accountable to answer before God. Sometime, somewhere, that is a key question that will measure and judge our lives. Now, we see that documented again here in this graphic parable in Luke 16, the parable of Dives, the rich man, and Lazarus, the poor beggar. It's important to note that this parable is not a geographical description of heaven and hell. It's a drama! It's like a one-act play with two scenes.

Scene 1 opens on an elegant dining room. The table is covered with food and graced with silver candlesticks. Dressed in luxurious purple splendor, Dives, the rich man (we know his name from tradition, though he is not named in the scriptures), sits there selfishly eating, indulging himself, unaware of and unconcerned about a world out there that may be hurting or hungry. Thus he eats and lives every day. Seated at the door is a poor, wretched beggar, the picture of misery and abject poverty, skin and bones, eyes sunk back, covered with sores.

His name is Lazarus. The unclean street dogs come and lick his sores, and he is so weak that he cannot ward them off or run them away. Lazarus is waiting for the bread that will be thrown his way from the rich man's table. Scholars tell us that in those days, people didn't have napkins, so they wiped their lips and chins and fingers with bread and then threw the bread aside. This was what Lazarus was waiting for, the thrown-away bread, as scene 1 comes to an end.

As the curtain goes up on scene 2, the tables are turned. The roles are completely reversed. Lazarus (the poor beggar) has now died and is in comfort in heaven, while Dives is in agony in hell. Dives, the rich man, pleads that Lazarus might be sent to earth as a miraculous messenger from the dead to warn his five brothers. But the answer comes back that the brothers have Moses and the prophets to look to for guidance, and that if they don't hear them, then they won't be convinced by someone rising from the dead. With that pronouncement the curtain closes, and the play ends.

But what does it mean? What do we make of this? What can we learn from this? What is Jesus trying to teach us here? That it's wrong to be rich? Of course not! We miss the point if we come to that conclusion. The sin of Dives was not in being wealthy. His sin was in not caring. His sin was his blind self-centeredness. His sin was his arrogant, indulgent apathy.

This is a tremendously relevant parable for our time because "the Dives Syndrome" is so dramatically with us today in what is called the epidemic of "me-ism." Go to the bookstore this week and notice the great number of books (many of them on the best-seller charts) that propose trendy techniques to get the most pleasure, power, and personal satisfaction out of life. The theme of many of these books is "me-ism"—"look out for number one" or "power by intimidation." The Dives Syndrome is still with us, extolling the virtues of selfishness.

Recently, I read about a young man who was applying for a job as an usher in a large theater. In the interview, the manager asked him the question, "What would you do if the theater suddenly caught on fire?" "Oh sir, you don't have to worry about me!" said the young man.

"I'm a survivor. I would be the first one out of there!" That was not the answer the manager was looking for!

In the NBC coverage of the 1988 Olympics, there was a fascinating human-interest story. A number of the athletes were asked this question: "Of all the great athletes in these Olympic Games, which one inspires and impresses you most?" Some said, "Greg Louganis." Some said, "Phoebe Mills." Others said, "Evelyn Ashford," "Edwin Moses," "Florence Griffith-Joyner," or "Carl Lewis." However, one boxer said (and I quote), "In all honesty, I'd pick *me*!" The Dives Syndrome of self-centeredness still haunts us.

What a narrow, limited way to live! Dives had a life limited, walled in, and shut off from the rest of the world by his own selfishness. He had a limited vision, a limited faith, and limited love. Let's take a look at these.

First, Dives's Problem Was That He Had a Limited Vision

Dives is not described as an evil person. There is no listing of vices here. His sin was not that he did cruel things to Lazarus. No, Dives's sin was that he did not see Lazarus! For him, Lazarus had become just another part of the landscape. Dives didn't see Lazarus anymore. He didn't hear his cry or feel his pain or see his plight. Dives had a limited vision.

In his book *Reshaping the Christian Life,** Robert Raines put it dramatically when he said:

> Hell is total preoccupation with self. Hell is the condition of being tone deaf to the word of grace, blind to the presence of God . . . and unable to discern His image in another person. Hell is that state in which we no longer catch the fragrance of life or breathe in the salt breeze of the Holy Spirit; when the taste buds of life are so dulled that there is no tang or sparkle to living. Hell is to live in the presence of love and not know it, not feel it, not be warmed by it. It is to live in the Father's house like the older son (Luke 15) but be insensitive to the Father's love. Hell is to be unaware of God's world, God's people, the reality of God in oneself; it is to be spiritually blind, it is to have the doors in life closed tight, to abide in one's own darkness.

(*Robert A. Raines, *Reshaping the Christian Life* [New York: Harper & Row, 1964], p. 90. Used by author's permission.)

*Robert Raines's most recent book is *A Time to Live: Seven Steps to Creative Aging.* Plume, published by the Penguin Group, New York, 1998.

Blinded by his own high lifestyle, Dives had forgotten how to see with his heart. Does that sound at all familiar? Could that happen to us? This is why the outreach program of the church is so important. We must never become "fat cats." We must never become a "silk stocking" church. As long as there are people on this globe who are hurting or hungry or sick or illiterate, then we cannot, we must not, look at the world with dry eyes.

Not long ago, I was trying to help a person who is homeless, someone who lives on the street. I asked him, "What is the hardest thing about your life here?" I expected him to say something about not having enough food to eat or a place to sleep, but his answer surprised me. He said, "The people don't look at me."

The world is our parish! The world is Lazarus at our doorstep. We must see the needy people of our congregations and our world with compassionate hearts and touch them with helping hands.

Antoine de Saint Exupéry, in his classic book *The Little Prince*, put it like this: "It is only with the heart that one can see rightly; what is essential is invisible to the eye" (Antoine de Saint-Exupéry, *The Little Prince.* Katherine Woods, trans. [New York: Reynal & Hitchcock, 1943], p. 70.)

That was a part of Dives' problem. He had a limited vision. He had closed his eyes to the needs of others. He had stopped seeing with his heart. He didn't see Lazarus anymore. Let me ask you something: How is your vision right now? Can you see other people with your heart? Dives couldn't, and that was part of his problem. He had a limited vision.

Second, Dives Had a Limited Faith

Dives had a faith limited by excesses, excuses, and alibis: Well, it's really all God's fault. If God had given me a sign, if he had sent me a miracle, I would have believed, thought Dives.

Dives had a limited faith, because he had an "artful alibi"—a half-baked excuse: *If God had just sent me a miracle, I would have believed!* And in addition, he thought that the only hope for his brothers was a messenger from the dead. That kind of shallow approach to faith has been around for a long time. Again and again, people said it to Jesus: "Give us a sign!" "Wow us with a miracle!" "If you are really the Christ, come off the cross, and we will believe!"

We look for God in the wrong places—in the strange, the unusual, the bizarre—when the truth is that God is closer than breathing, nearer than hands and feet. As Elizabeth Barrett Browning once put it,

> *Earth's crammed with heaven,*
> *And every common bush afire with God;*
> *But only he who sees, takes off his shoes,*
> *The rest sit round it and pluck blackberries.*

("Aurora Leigh," 1856)

Excuse-making is a tactic we learn early. We try to "excuse" ourselves by placing the blame on somebody else or by creating an alibi that we think will let us off the hook.

For example, one Saturday morning some years ago, I was standing by the kitchen sink when our son, Jeff, came "karate-chopping" his way into the room. Jeff was six years old at the time and was going through a stage where he was "karate-chopping" everything in sight. He karate-chopped the breakfast table, the chairs, and the refrigerator.

But when he karate-chopped the dishwasher, he accidentally hit the ON button. When the dishwasher started up, Jeff stopped abruptly in his tracks.

He knew he had done something he shouldn't have, but quickly rose to the occasion. He looked at me and said, "It's okay, Dad. We'll tell Mom you did it!"

So early in life it happens, we develop the ability to make creative excuses and alibis because sometimes it is so difficult to face up to the truth.

That is precisely what we see Dives doing here in this parable: trying to excuse himself. Dives had a limited faith because (like many of us) he was always looking for an alibi or a way to excuse his actions or to justify his inactions. "If God had just sent me a miracle, I would have believed!"

No handwriting in the sky, no ghosts from the dead, no cosmic miracles, no lightning bolts from heaven. But really, when you stop to think about it, God has indeed given us a special sign. God wrapped his sign, his message, up in a person, and in effect, said, "Here it is! This is what I want you to be like! This is how I want you to act! This is how I want you to live! This is my message, and your Savior!"

Jesus shows us the way to abundant life and mature faith. Dives had a limited vision and a limited faith.

Third and Finally, Dives Had a Limited Love

Dives loved his family and his friends. He loved those who loved him back. He loved those who could do things for him, but his love was limited, exclusive, measured. He parceled it out to only a choice few. He didn't love Lazarus. He didn't love the poor, the needy, the lowly, the outcast. He didn't love those people who were different from him.

I have a psychologist friend who advises her patients to treat every person they meet each day as if he or she were the most important person in the world. I like that, but you know, the Christian faith takes it a step farther, a giant step farther! The Christian faith tells us to relate to every single person we meet as if that person were Christ, himself, in disguise! Think about that. More than that, let me invite you to try it! If you will earnestly try that, to love every single person you meet as if that person were Christ in disguise, if you would try that for one day, it will change your life forever!

6
The Unmerciful Servant:
Lord, Help Me Forgive

Scripture: Matthew 18:21-22, 23-35

Kids say the most wonderful things, especially our granddaughter, Sarah. She is eleven years old now, in the fifth grade at school, and she is continually coming up with these always fascinating and often humorous "quotable quotes."

Just last week, I was talking to Jodi, our daughter and Sarah's mother, on the telephone. It was 8:30 at night. Jodi told me that Sarah had experienced a full day—school, then gymnastics, and then softball practice. Jodi said, "Sarah is so tired. She's sitting here on the floor, about to fall asleep sitting up." Sarah overheard this. She always overhears everything. And Sarah said, "Momma, it's not the softball. It's those hormones kicking in!"

I don't know about you, but I don't think I even heard the word *hormones* till I was in college. Kids do say the most wonderful things.

Recently I was visiting with a little girl named Rachel, who is five years old. She was showing me her Bible storybook and telling me that her mother reads her a Bible story every night. "Which story is your favorite?" I asked her. Quick as a flash she answered, "My favorite one is the one where the king forgives his servant, but the servant doesn't forgive his coworker." I was surprised. I had fully expected her to say David and Goliath, or the Prodigal Son, or the Good Samaritan, or Zacchaeus. But no, instead she picked the parable of the unmerciful servant, from Matthew 18.

Intrigued, I said to her, "Rachel, why is that story your all-time favorite?" Rachel replied, "I like that one best of all because it teaches us that God is nice, and he wants us to be nice!"

Out of the mouths of little children! Rachel was right on target, wasn't she? That is precisely

what Jesus is teaching us in this great parable
in Matthew 18:

God is loving, and he wants us to be loving.
God is gracious, and he wants us to be
gracious.
God is forgiving, and he wants us to be
forgiving.
God is merciful, and he wants us to merciful.
God is compassionate, and he wants us to be
compassionate.

Or as five-year-old Rachel might put it, "God
is nice to us, and he wants us to be nice to each
other!" The scriptures are very clear about this.
When it comes to forgiveness, we as Christians
are called to imitate the forgiving spirit of God.
The scriptures point out very dramatically that
we are to forgive others as graciously, as lov-
ingly, as mercifully, as thoroughly as God in
Christ forgives us. Jesus sums it up in Luke 6
when he says, "Be merciful, just as your Father
is merciful" (v. 36). And here in Matthew 18, in
the parable of the unmerciful servant, Jesus
underscores again the importance of the forgiving spirit. Remember the parable with me. It's
like a one-act play with three scenes. It illustrates graphically the power and beauty of

forgiveness, and it exposes dramatically the ugliness of the unforgiving spirit.

In Scene 1, a servant is brought before the king. This servant owes the king an astounding debt, ten thousand talents, a humongous debt—or in contemporary terms, ten million dollars. Let me put that in perspective this way: In that time, a young slave could be bought for one talent, about a thousand dollars, and this servant owes the king 10,000 talents; that sum would buy 10,000 slaves. If this debt were put into coins, it would take 8,600 people to carry it all, with each carrying 60 pounds of coins, and the carriers would form a line 5 miles long. We are talking big money here! (Statistics adapted from Barclay, *The Daily Study Bible, The Gospel of Matthew*, pp. 213-14.)

Also, at this time, the total amount of the annual taxes for the five geographical regions of Judea, Idumea, Samaria, Galilee, and Perea, all totaled together, came to only 800 talents; and here this one servant owes 10,000 talents, millions of dollars, and he can't possibly pay it back. Talk about "amazing grace"! Look what happens here.

The man acknowledges his enormous debt, and he pleads for mercy. Incredibly, the king, who is a gracious man, is moved with compassion, and his heart goes out to this servant. The king cancels the debt, he lets the servant off the hook, and he forgives him and sets him free.

In the second scene, the shoe is on the other foot. The man who has just been forgiven this enormous debt of ten million dollars walks out of the palace and immediately sees a fellow servant who owes him twenty dollars. What does he do? He grabs this man by the throat and says, "Pay me what you owe. Give me my twenty dollars now." The fellow servant falls to his knees and pleads for mercy, but the unmerciful servant, who only moments before received incredible forgiveness from the gracious king, has no mercy to give. There is no forgiveness in his heart, and he sends his coworker to debtors' prison.

Here in scene 2, we see the graphic ugliness of the unforgiving spirit. Here we see in a dramatic way how ungrateful and mixed up we can become when we accept God's gracious forgiveness and then refuse to forgive others, refuse to live in that spirit, refuse to pass it on to others.

In the final scene, the king is again center stage. A group of servants come to him filled with distress. They report what the unmerciful servant has done. The king is not happy. He calls in the unmerciful servant and rebukes him: "What's this I hear? I forgave your debt. Should you not have had the same kind of mercy on your fellow servant?" Then the king casts the unmerciful servant into prison, and the curtain comes down and the play is over, but the message lingers and haunts.

Let me ask you a very personal question: Are you at odds with anybody? Are you estranged, distanced, cut off from anybody? Has someone hurt you? Are you having a hard time forgiving that person? Are you finding it hard to forgive? If so, let me make three suggestions about what you can do, three practical and biblical suggestions. Here's number one.

First of All, Recognize Your Own Need of Forgiveness

There is an interesting story about a woman in a large city who left her suburban apartment one morning for a trip downtown on the bus. She put on one of her most fashionable outfits and her favorite perfume, and headed out the side door to catch Bus # 49, which would transport her to the best shopping district in town. As she hurried out the backdoor, she had a last-minute thought to pick up a small sack of garbage that had accumulated in the kitchen, and to toss it into the container at the curb on her way to catch the bus. However, she became preoccupied and forgot she had the sack of garbage in her hand, along with her other packages, and she lugged the garbage unwittingly onto the bus.

Immediately as she took her seat, she noticed this terrible stench. She became upset with the city and determined then and there to write an angry letter protesting this awful odor on this city bus. She opened the window, but still the stench was there, and she decided that the neighborhood through which she was riding just smelled awful. "Some people just don't know how to live," she muttered to herself. "They just aren't very clean."

When she arrived at the shopping district, she discovered that horrible stench in every single store she visited. "The whole world smells terrible. The whole world is going to the dogs," she complained.

When she finally returned home and opened her packages, only then did she realize where the terrible odor was coming from!

Maybe we would be more inclined to forgive others if we first recognized the garbage we are carrying around in our own lives. The great

African American spiritual puts it like this: "It's me, it's me, it's me, O Lord, standing in the need of prayer. Not my brother, not my sister, but it's me, O Lord, standing in the need of prayer."

It happened in the football locker room. I was in the tenth grade at the time. Some of the players were griping and complaining and bashing one of our teammates named Tim. Tim had dropped a pass in the end zone. We had lost the game, and the players were crucifying Tim behind his back with hard, angry words. "Tim cost us the game!" "It's all his fault!" "Anybody could have caught that ball!" "He's terrible!" "If I were the coach, I would kick him off the team!" "He's a coward! He dropped it because he's so scared!"

On and on they went, ripping Tim apart. All except a senior named George. He just sat there quietly, slowly unlacing his football shoes. Suddenly the others noticed that George was not participating in the verbal massacre of Tim. George was one of the most highly respected players on the team. They tried to involve him in the cruel gossip. "Hey, George, wasn't that terrible how Tim lost the game for us?" I'll never forget how George handled that. He said, "You know, I have way too many faults of my own to be critical of anybody else, and besides that, I imagine that right about now Tim feels worse than any of us."

That promptly ended the cruel bashing session, and it also revealed why George was one of the most highly respected players on the team.

If we ever have a hard time forgiving someone who has done something hurtful to us, it helps to remember that the first step is to recognize our own clay feet, our own need to be forgiven.

That comes first: to recognize our own need to be forgiven.

Second, Accept God's Gracious Forgiveness

God's forgiveness is available to us, but he won't force it on us. We have to accept it.

Some years ago, Bishop Willis J. King told a true story that touched me greatly. Bishop King was the first African American bishop to get a Ph.D. in Old Testament in America. Upon his graduation from Wiley College, he went back home to spend a few days with his parents. He showed them his degree. He was so proud of it. Then he announced, "Tomorrow morning first thing, I'm going to go to the downtown bank and I'm going to borrow $500 to buy my first automobile."

The next morning, as he was about to leave, his father said to him, "Son, don't you want me to go with you and co-sign your note?" He said, "No, Dad, I can take care of this by myself. I've got my degree now."

The officer at the bank said, "So you want to borrow $500. Tell me, what do you have for collateral? If you're going to get $500 from this bank, you've got to have something of equal value." "Oh, yes sir," Bishop King said, "I've got my degree—a Ph.D. degree!" The bank officer said, "I'm sorry, but we can't use that degree as collateral for $500 in this bank. I'm afraid you'll have to go elsewhere."

Bishop King said he felt embarrassed, humiliated, and defeated. But then he heard a familiar voice. His dad had come to help him, and he said, "Son, I've come to co-sign your note." "But Dad," he said, "you can't even write. All you can do is make an 'X'." And the banker said, "Son, it may be true that your dad can't write, and all he can do is make an 'X.' But I want to tell you something, it's that 'X' that got the loan to get you into school. It's that 'X' that got the loan to get you out of school. And if you are going to get a loan today from this bank to buy a new car, it's that same 'X' that's going to get that for you!"

Bishop King summed up the story like this. He said, "In that moment, I realized something more powerfully than ever before, namely, how inadequate I am, how needy I am, how insufficient I am alone, and how on Calvary's cross, Jesus co-signed my note! I wouldn't be here tonight if he hadn't. Love lifted me. When nothing else could help, love lifted me. Jesus signed my note, and I accepted that gift that only he can give." (This story was told by Zan Holmes, the Shamblin Lecturer at St. Luke's United Methodist Church, Houston, 1991.)

If we want to be able to forgive, first we need to recognize our own need of forgiveness; second, we need to accept God's gracious gift of forgiveness.

Third and Finally, We Pass On That Forgiveness to Others

We do this by living daily in the spirit of forgiveness. We become the instruments of God's love and peace. We become conduits of his grace and mercy.

In the book and movie *The Hiding Place,* Corrie ten Boom tells of her suffering in German concentration camps during World War II. Miraculously, Corrie ten Boom survived that horrendous experience, and after the war she traveled extensively, speaking and telling of God's grace through those horrible years.

On one occasion in Munich, a man came up to her after she finished speaking, and she recognized him. He had been a prison guard in Ravensbruck, a man who had been so cruel to her and her sister. He did not recognize her. He extended his hand to Corrie ten Boom, and he said, "How grateful I am for your message, Fraulein. To think, as you say, 'He has washed my sins away.'"

All the horrible memories of the past flooded into her mind. She struggled to raise her hand, but it wouldn't move; it remained at her side. "Forgive me, Lord, and help me forgive him," she prayed. Nothing happened. Again she prayed, "Jesus, I cannot forgive him. Give me your forgiveness." Corrie ten Boom describes what happened next like this: "As I took his hand the most incredible thing happened. From my shoulder along my arm and through my hand, a current seemed to pass from me to him, while into my heart sprang a love . . . that almost overwhelmed me" (Corrie ten Boom, *The Hiding Place*, Bantam Books, New York, 1974, p. 238).

Has someone been cruel to you? Has someone hurt you deeply? Maybe you feel that there's no way you could ever forgive that person, and on your own strength you probably can't. But you can ask Christ to give you his forgiveness. You can ask for his help. Let the power of his forgiveness flow through you. Let his gracious spirit be your spirit. That's how it works. We recognize our need of forgiveness, we accept God's gracious forgiveness, and we pass on that forgiveness to others.

Study Guide

John D. Schroeder

This book by James W. Moore examines six of the parables of Jesus that contain direction and truth for making the most out of life. To assist you in facilitating a discussion group, this study guide was created to help make this experience beneficial for both you and members of your group. Here are some thoughts on how you can help your group:

1. Distribute the book to participants before your first meeting and request that they come having read the brief introduction and the first

chapter. You may want to limit the size of your group to increase participation.

2. Begin your sessions on time. Your participants will appreciate your promptness. You may wish to begin your first session with introductions and a brief get-acquainted time. Start each session by reading aloud the snapshot summary of the chapter for the day.

3. Select discussion questions and activities in advance. Note that the first question is a general question designed to get discussion going. The last question is designed to summarize the discussion. Feel free to change the order of the listed questions and to create your own questions. Allow a set amount of time for the questions and activities.

4. Remind your participants that all questions are valid as part of the learning process. Encourage their participation in discussion by saying that there are no "wrong" answers and that all input will be appreciated. Invite participants to share their thoughts, personal stories, and ideas as their comfort level allows.

5. Some questions may be more difficult to answer than others. If you ask a question and no one responds, begin the discussion by venturing an answer yourself. Then ask for comments and other answers. Remember

that some questions may have multiple answers.

6. Ask the question "Why?" or "Why do you believe that?" to help continue a discussion and give it greater depth.

7. Give everyone a chance to talk. Keep the conversation moving. Occasionally you may want to direct a question to a specific person who has been quiet. "Do you have anything to add?" is a good follow-up question to ask another person. If the topic of conversation gets off track, move ahead by asking the next question in your study guide.

8. Before moving from questions to activities, ask group members if they have any questions that have not been answered. Remember that as a leader, you do not have to know all the answers. Some answers may come from group members. Other answers may even need a bit of research. Your job is to keep the discussion moving and to encourage participation.

9. Review the activity in advance. Feel free to modify it or to create your own activity. Encourage participants to try the "At home" activity.

10. Following the conclusion of the activity, close with a brief prayer, praying either the

printed prayer from the study guide or a prayer of your own. If your group desires, pause for individual prayer petitions.

11. Be grateful and supportive. Thank group members for their ideas and participation.

12. You are not expected to be a "perfect" leader. Just do the best you can by focusing on the participants and the lesson. God will help you lead this group.

13. Enjoy your time together!

Suggestions for Participants

1. What you will receive from this study will be in direct proportion to your involvement. Be an active participant!

2. Please make it a point to attend all sessions and to arrive on time so that you can receive the greatest benefit.

3. Read the chapter and review the study-guide questions prior to the meeting. You may want to jot down questions you have from the reading and also answers to some of the study-guide questions.

4. Be supportive and appreciative of your group leader as well as the other members of your group. You are on a journey together.

5. Your participation is encouraged. Feel free

to share your thoughts about the material being discussed.

6. Pray for your group and your leader.

Chapter 1
The Laborers in God's Vineyard

Snapshot Summary

1. God is generous and wants us to be generous as well.

2. There is no place in God's kingdom for resentment.

3. There is no place in God's kingdom for selfishness.

4. There is no place in God's kingdom for arrogance.

Reflection / Discussion Questions

1. How does this parable speak to you? How is it relevant to your life today?

2. What does this parable say about God and God's kingdom?

3. What does the author say is the first key to this parable (found in Matthew 20:1), and what truth does it unlock?

4. In your own words, what does it mean to be generous?

5. Explain how resentment damages us and others.

6. What does the author say is the second key to this parable (found in Matthew 20:15), and what truth does it unlock?

7. What are some of the causes of selfishness? How are we hurt when we are selfish?

8. Give your definition of *arrogance,* and an example of it.

9. Explain and compare the concerns of the householder and the concerns of the workers.

10. Why is this parable a good illustration of God's character and love for us?

11. What do we learn from this parable about fairness?

12. Make a list of some of the practical applications for living found in this parable.

Activities

As a group: As a group or as individuals, create one or more bumper-sticker slogans that communicate a message from this parable in eight words or less.

At home: Perform a generous act this week that shows unconditional love.

Prayer: *Dear God, thank you for showing us what it means to be generous. Help us to block resentment, selfishness, and arrogance from our lives, and to be giving, fair, and loving in all that we do. Just as you have been generous to us, help us to pass along that generosity to others. May we be faithful workers as we strive to build your kingdom. Amen.*

Chapter 2
The Pharisee and the Publican

Snapshot Summary

1. We need to be plugged in to gratitude.
2. We need to be plugged in to generosity.
3. We need to be plugged in to God.

Reflection / Discussion Questions

1. Why did Jesus tell this parable? What messages did he want to get across?

2. Share a time when you felt the power of God.

3. What does it cost to be grateful to or generous with others?

4. Reflect on / discuss why it is important to

be grateful. How does gratitude benefit both the giver and the receiver?

5. How are we sometimes like the Pharisee in this parable?

6. Reflect on / talk about a time when someone was generous to you. How did it make you feel?

7. Reflect on / discuss some practical applications of this parable to our daily lives.

8. What qualities please God? How do we know this?

9. What does it mean to "get plugged in to God"? How does this occur?

10. How can the Bible help us get plugged in to God?

11. What causes some people to have a "power failure" and not be connected to God?

12. In what ways does this parable challenge you?

Activities

As a group: Create a list of things you can accomplish when you plug in to God, considering the accessibility of God's power and presence.

At home: Make today the start of your own personal "Count Your Blessings Week"! Make it a point each day this week to count the many blessings you have received from God and from others. Strive to be a blessing to others this week!

Prayer: *Dear God, thank you for the opportunity to learn what you desire for us. Help us to show genuine gratitude and generosity to others each day of our lives. May we share your love with others. Remind us of your unending power and presence, and may we remain connected to you. Amen.*

Chapter 3
The Weeds Among the Wheat

Snapshot Summary

1. Overreaction can cause you to lose your temper.

2. Overreaction can cause you to lose your marriage.

3. Overreaction can cause you to lose your church or your spiritual balance.

Reflection / Discussion Questions

1. Share some ideas about how this parable has practical applications for us today.

2. Reflect on / discuss a time when you over-reacted to a situation. What caused your over-reaction?

3. Review and briefly reflect on / discuss the five observations made by the author concerning this parable.

4. Give some reasons why people lose their temper. What kind of damage can be caused by a lost temper?

5. Reflect on / discuss the difference between *reacting* and *responding* when it comes to people in a relationship.

6. List some reasons why people drop out of church. Who is at fault when someone drops out, and why?

7. What does this parable tell us about God?

8. Explain what it means to lose your spiritual balance. What are some warning signs that you are losing your spiritual balance?

9. Name a person you admire who does not overreact, and describe how this person handles tough situations.

10. What are some of the dangers of "overcorrecting" in an attempt to solve a problem? What would be an example of overcorrection?

11. List some judgments people are not capable of making or should not make. Give some examples.

12. How does this parable challenge you?

Activities

As a group: Ask each person to take a sheet of paper and a pen or pencil, and write down about five ideas on creative and unique ways to prevent overreaction. Share the ideas with the group.

At home: Focus this week on responding rather than reacting. Put this into practice at home and at the office. See what a difference it makes.

Prayer: *Dear God, thank you for reminding us that there are always weeds among the wheat. We live in an imperfect world that challenges us not to lose our temper or our balance. Help us to look to Jesus as the example of how to live and to love. Help us to respond, and not to react in haste or without knowing the facts. Grant us patience and wisdom to live as your children. Amen.*

Chapter 4
The Ten Pounds

Snapshot Summary

1. We can be immobilized or destroyed by our appetites.

2. We can be immobilized or destroyed by our attitudes.

3. We can be immobilized or destroyed by our anxieties.

Reflection / Discussion Questions

1. What new insights did you gain from reading this chapter?

2. Think about and name both professions and people who use their gifts to help you.

3. Share a time when you battled competing desires within you both to pull back and to move forward.

4. Explain what it means to be frozen by appetites. Give an example.

5. In your own words, explain what it means to have a destructive attitude.

6. Reflect on / discuss the statement that "how we feel about God greatly affects how we feel about life."

7. List some of the causes and cures of a bad attitude.

8. Share a time when you were frozen by anxiety.

9. Which causes more grief for you—your appetites, attitudes, or anxieties? Explain.

10. What additional things can cause us to freeze up on our faith pilgrimage?

11. Name some strategies for overcoming the fear that can immobilize us.

12. Compile a list of lessons and practical applications we can learn from this parable.

Activities

As a group: Create a list of things that we lose if we don't use them. Include in your list lost opportunities for helping others, and examples of how others lose if we don't get involved.

At home: Just like in the parable, you have been given talents. This week, make an inventory of your talents that God has given you. Consider what use you are making of your talents.

Prayer: *Dear God, thank you for the gifts and talents you have given each of us. Help us to be good servants and to use these talents wisely, so that they may help others and bring glory to you. Guide us so that we are not destroyed by our appetites, our attitudes, or our anxieties. Grant us direction on our faith pilgrimage so that we may walk with you in love all the days of our lives. Amen.*

Chapter 5
Dives and Lazarus

Snapshot Summary

1. Caring means having unlimited vision.
2. Caring means having unlimited faith.
3. Caring means having unlimited love.

Reflection / Discussion Questions

1. What new insights did you gain from reading this chapter?

2. Why did Jesus tell this parable? What lessons does it hold for us today?

3. What examples of Lazarus do you see in our world today? What examples do you see of Dives?

4. What was the sin of Dives? How is "the Dives Syndrome"—the attitude of "look out for number one" or power by intimidation—still with us today? Give an example.

5. How many opportunities for caring would you say the average person has each day?

6. What sometimes prevents us from caring?

7. List some ways in which we can be more caring and sensitive to the needs of others.

8. Explain how Dives had limited vision. How might we have the same problem?

9. List some of the symptoms of having a limited faith.

10. What does it cost to be a caring person? What sacrifices must sometimes be made?

11. Who taught you a lesson in caring as a child or was a model for you? How have they influenced your life?

12. What is the importance of treating every single person we meet as if that person were Christ, and what does this have to do with love?

Activities

As a group: Brainstorm ideas for a group service project that will benefit persons who are poor or in need. Schedule a time and a date to do this project as a group.

At home: Increase your caring quotient! Strive to perform daily acts of caring this week.

Prayer: *Dear God, thank you for giving us the vision, faith, and love we need to care for others. Help us to put these gifts into action for the benefit of those who need our love and* compassion. *Show us how to step out in faith and move beyond our comfort zones to address the needs of others. Remind us that you are always with us, and that you have given us the strength and ability to be your hands and voice in this world. Amen.*

Chapter 6
The Unmerciful Servant

Snapshot Summary

1. We need to recognize our own need for forgiveness.

2. We need to accept God's gracious forgiveness.

3. We need to pass on God's forgiveness to others.

Reflection / Discussion Questions

1. What new insights did you gain from reading this chapter?

2. Share a time when you received forgiveness. Describe how it feels to be forgiven.

3. List some of the common mistakes in life for which we need forgiveness.

4. Why is it important to recognize your own need for forgiveness?

5. List some of the reasons why people withhold forgiveness from others.

6. What lessons about God do we learn from this parable?

7. In what ways are we sometimes like the unmerciful servant?

8. Explain how we often hurt ourselves when we fail to forgive and forget.

9. What do we need to do in order to gain God's forgiveness?

10. In your own words, explain what it means to forgive someone.

11. Is it simple to forgive or is it complicated? Explain your answer.

12. In what situations would forgiveness be the most difficult to offer?

Activities

As a group: Share your thoughts and feelings about the impact the lessons in this book have had upon you. How have you been changed or challenged?

At home: Practice a spirit of forgiveness this week. Seek to be a healer.

Prayer: *Dear God, thank you for your gracious gift of forgiveness. As your children, help us to extend this gift to others. Show us how to be loving and kind to every person we come into contact with each day. In Jesus' name. Amen.*